QUESTIONS KIDS WISH THEY COULD ASK THEIR PARENTS

Zoe Stern
AND Ellen Sue Stern

Handlettered & Illustrated by Toni Tajima

CELESTIAL ARTS
BERKELEY, CALIFORNIA

Handlettered text and illustrations copyright © 1993 by Toni Tajima

CA
Celestial Arts
P.O. Box 7327
Berkeley, California 94707

First printing 1993

Library of Congress cataloging-in-publication data
Stern, Zoe.
   Questions kids wish they could ask their parents / by Zoe Stern and Ellen Sue Stern.
      p.   cm.
   ISBN 0-89087-692-4
     1. Parent and Child. 2. Parenting. 3. Child rearing.   I. Stern, Ellen Sue, 1954 —   . II. Title
   HQ755.85.S74   1993
   306.874 -- dc20
                                                                    93-6804
                                                                    CIP

1 2 3 4 5 6 - 98 97 96 95 94 93   Printed in the U.S.A.

I dedicate this book to Uri Allen and Nanny Jane
Zoe

This book is dedicated with great love, to my daughter, Zoe.
Ellen Sue

ACKNOWLEDGMENTS

We wish to thank the following individuals: David Hinds and Fuzzy Randall for making this a ton of fun; Johnathon Lazear for your ongoing support; Beverly Lewis for your encouragment and feedback; Mab Nulty for your creative help; the students at Susan Lindgren School who participated in the focus groups; Jason Rodich, Brian Marks, Joey Morris, Jessie and Jill Edelstein, and Natalie Fursetzer for your friendship; Gary Stern for your wonderful input; and last, but not least, Evan Stern, Zoe's little brother, for all your patience and help.

TABLE OF CONTENTS

♦ INTRODUCTION — 1

♦ FOREWORD — 3

♦ WHY NOT ? — 9

♦ WHY DO YOU MAKE EVERYTHING SEEM SO WONDERFUL WHEN IT ISN'T ? — 11

♦ ARE YOU SCARED OF THE MONSTERS IN YOUR CLOSET ? — 14

♦ WHY DO YOU JUMP TO CONCLUSIONS WITHOUT HEARING MY SIDE OF THE STORY ? — 21

♦ DID DADDY GET THAT LOAN HE NEEDED FOR HIS BUSINESS ? — 24

♦ WHY ARE YOU ALWAYS TOO BUSY TO PLAY WITH ME ? — 27

♦ WHY DO SOME PEOPLE NOT LIKE IT THAT I'm JEWISH ? — 30

♦ WHY DIDN'T YOU ASK ME IF I WANTED A LITTLE BROTHER ? — 33

◆ WHY DID YOU AND DADDY GET DIVORCED ?   37

◆ WHY WON'T YOU LET ME GO TO THE MALL WITH MY
   FRIENDS ?   40

◆ DID I EVER DO SOMETHING TO MAKE YOU NOT LOVE ME?   43

◆ WHY DO YOU YELL SO MUCH ?   47

◆ DO YOUR RICE KRISPIES TALK TO YOU ?   51

◆ WHEN WILL DADDY START WEARING HIS SEATBELT ?   55

◆ DO YOU THINK I'M POPULAR ?   57

◆ HAVE YOU EVER HAD SEX ?   59

◆ WHY CAN'T I PUT YOU IN TIME OUT ?   61

◆ WHY ARE YOU SO NOSY ?   65

◆ WHY DO YOU MAKE ME READ BOOKS ABOUT SEX
   AND PERIODS ?   69

◆ WAS I A MISTAKE ?   72

◆ WHY DO YOU MAKE ME WEAR THINGS I HATE?   75

◆ WOULD YOU LOVE ME IF I WAS DUMB?   79

◆ ARE YOU AFRAID TO DIE?   82

◆ WHEN WILL YOU STOP SMOKING?   85

◆ IF GOD CAN SEE EVERYTHING WHY DOESN'T HE
   TELL ME WHEN MY BROTHER'S ABOUT TO TRASH
   MY ROOM?   87

· INTRODUCTION ·

I'm writing this book because I'm a child and I care about children. I've seen good parents, great parents, and not-so-great parents. I've seen lots of things that make me sad and mad — parents who grab their kids in shopping malls, parents who don't listen when their kids try to tell them things, parents who hit their kids and other bad things that make me want to get parents to stop and think about what they're doing. Otherwise, kids can grow up and hurt their own kids and that would be a terrible thing. QUESTIONS KIDS WISH THEY COULD ASK THEIR PARENTS will help parents know what's on their kids minds so they can love and

1

and respect each other more. I hope you pay attention to what's in this book so that you can be a great parent. a great parent.

Good luck

Zoe Stern

⬩ FOREWORD ⬩

So, the first question you're probably asking yourself is, "Did a child REALLY write this book?"
The answer is Yes.
And No. Well, not all by herself.

This book evolved out of a series of mother/daughter heart-to-heart talks; the kinds we have while we're driving in the car on the way to the supermarket or hanging out at the dinner table waiting for The Simpsons to start. Those spontaneous, meaningful conversations that happen when we least expect them and we think about for a long time afterward.
Conversations about life. And death. About sex,

manners, clothes, bedtime, AIDS, homework, and whether life was easier back in the "olden days" before there were microwaves, Nintendo, and 25 flavors of Häagen-Dazs.

Since both I and Zoe's father are published authors, it seemed natural to translate these conversations into a book. Doing so gave our daughter a personal glimpse into another side of her parents' lives; in the process, she forever changed mine.

I learned a lot about my daughter —and myself— as we set out to explore these topics together. We began in the summer, spending Saturday afternoons wearing matching berets, writing at Cafe Weird. As the autumn chill set in, we curled up under a

4

blanket in front of the fire; Zoe sipping hot choco-late while I drank mug after mug of coffee.

These were intimate conversations. Here's how they usually went:

E.S.: "Okay, Zoe, let's talk about discipline today." She'd glare at me, then we'd commiserate at how tough it was to get started, especially tackling "hard topics," which most of them were.

E.S.: "So what's the best way for parents to disci-pline their kids?

Zoe: "Probably time-out. But they should never, never hit!"

E.S.: "Why not?"

Zoe: "Because it's wrong."

ES: "Wrong, how?"

Zoe: "It makes kids scared and teaches THEM to hit."

ES: "Why do you think parents do it, then?"

Zoe: "They're probably tired and frustrated... maybe their kids should put THEM in time-out..."

And on and on we'd go, diving in from all sides, trying our best to understand each others' point of view.

Sometimes we laughed and laughed. Other times, we'd wrestle and fight, when a topic hit

6

a nerve or touched on a conflict we were already embroiled in. And a few times we cried, sorting through our feelings about our families' divorce or reliving her beloved Papa Lester's death.

Throughout, I gained enormous respect for my daughter's stunning sensitivity, creativity, and courage to plumb the emotional depths of her being in order to get at the truth.

I'm very proud of what we've created together. This has been a true collaboration. And I hope it will be read by you and your children together. In the spirit it was written — as one of those sometimes excruciating, always enlightening — heart-to-heart talks.

Ellen Sue Stern

WHY NOT?

"Because" isn't a good enough answer.

When you just say, "because," it makes kids feel like they're not a person. For example, if your kid asks you, "Can I go to the movies?" and you say "no" and they say "why?" and you say "because" and they say "because why?" and you say "because I said so," they have no idea why you said "no" in the first place.

Instead you can say: "Because we have other plans tonight. Maybe another time."

9

Parents say, "because", because it's quick and easy.

But it isn't really because we'll just keep asking why and you won't be able to get any work done.

• SMART TALK:

Instead of saying, "Do it because I said so", say, "Do it because _____" and make sure you have a good reason.

 You're right, Zoe. You deserve a better answer than "because". But we don't always have one. Maybe if parents believed that "I don't know" was an okay answer, we wouldn't say "because".

WHY DO YOU MAKE EVERYTHING SEEM SO WONDERFUL WHEN IT ISN'T?

When something's wrong, Moms and Dads say: "It's nothing." But kids know it's not nothing... it's something.

Like when your kid falls down and has to go to the hospital and the parents say "Honey it's okay" but the parent has that LOOK on their face and you can tell it's not okay.

Or they say something under their breath but smile at you. This happens a lot at the doctor's. Parents say, "Oh, that won't hurt a bit... close your eyes and count to three..." Oh Yeah!!! Now you're really mad because they didn't tell the truth.

Parents seem to lie a lot. Like if there's a big storm and you have to go to your basement and your parents take out games and pretzels and pretend it's a party when you've seen the weather report and you know there's a tornado coming.

It's better to be prepared because then you won't freak out if your house blows down.

It's better to tell kids the truth...but then there's the Tooth Fairy and Santa Claus...

If your kid asks if you're the Tooth Fairy, keep them going as long as you can cause life should be magic.

But if they keep asking... especially if they're ten... tell them the truth. Because my parents said they weren't the Tooth Fairy and then I found a box of my old little teeth in my dad's sock drawer.

 If you're so sure I'm the Tooth Fairy why do you keep putting your teeth under the pillow?

13

ARE YOU SCARED OF THE MONSTERS IN YOUR CLOSET?

I am.

Don't ever laugh at your child's fears. Even if you think they're funny.

Kids are afraid of lots of things: Monsters, the dark, closets, war, throwing up, and things that look scary. The lamp in your bedroom can make a shadow that looks like a horrid blob with orange hair and a green face. Kids can imagine ANYTHING!

And we have nightmares. They don't always make sense. We'll come to you and even if you're tired or

14

frustrated or asleep, you HAVE to listen.

When we have nightmares, we need you to hug us and cuddle us and get us something to drink. Then tuck us back in bed and stay in the room and rub our backs until we fall asleep. Ask if we want to tell you about the nightmare. If we say "no", fine. If we want to, you need to pay attention even if it's boring.

Kids are also scared of robbers, kidnappers, tornados, raccoons, tigers, and our parents dying.

And sometimes we don't know what we're scared of. So don't say: "What are you scared of?" Because we might just not know. We might just be scared for no reason at all.

16

One thing that helps kids with scary feelings are dolls, blankets and other stuff they can hold on to. It's best if it's soft. Some kids call their blanket by another name. My daddy used to call his Mommick. Mine was called Beenite and I just gave it up two years ago.

Don't ever make fun of your child if he or she drags around a blanket or dolly. Same goes for pacifiers. Sucking thumbs or pacifiers helps kids feel safe. It also helps us fall asleep.

If you put nail polish or some other icky tasting stuff on their fingers so they won't suck them, at least tell your kid why. Admit that it's because YOU'RE embarrassed and don't like it.

I think that every kid needs to have something to suck on. Even if your kid still sucks their thumb when they're your age, that's up to them.

- ## DO'S AND DON'TS

DO let your child hold on to something.
DON'T make them feel bad about it.

DO allow them to bring it on outings.
DON'T be embarrassed.

DO let them choose when to give it up.
DON'T push it.

DO say how good it is when they give it up.
DON'T bribe.

It helps to know what kids are scared of. And it might help you to know that parents are scared too — and of some of the very same things. Know that when you're scared you can always crawl into my arms and I'll rock you back to sleep.

KIDS FEEL LIKE KINGS AND QUEENS
WHEN PARENTS RESPECT THEM

WHY DO YOU JUMP TO CONCLUSIONS WITHOUT HEARING MY SIDE OF THE STORY?

At my house we have family meetings where we discuss our problems. Everyone gets to say what they're feeling in the way they want to say it. Family meetings are fair. The parents aren't always in charge. And they're not always right. Sometimes kids are right. Sometimes both are right, but they just don't agree.

When parents are wrong the should say, "I'm sorry". That makes kids feel better. Respected.

Everyone in the family should have a vote, but

parents should have two because they're older and know more. Kids need to be heard, but we really don't want to be in charge. It makes us feel more secure knowing that parents will make the right decision.

• RESPECTFUL RULES:

1. LISTEN. When parents don't listen or act like they're listening when they're doing two things at once, kids feel hurt.

2. BE POLITE. When parents don't say please and thank-you, but expect their kids to, it's not fair.

3. BE KIND. When parents make fun of their kids

or don't take them seriously, it makes us feel stupid.

4. INCLUDE. When parents talk about their kids as if we're not on the face of the earth, when of course we can hear every word, it makes us feel invisible.

 Parents SHOULD listen more. Because sometimes kids are right and we don't want to admit it. Being in charge is hard. We don't always know what's best, all we can do is try to make good decisions.

DID DADDY GET THAT LOAN HE NEEDED FOR HIS BUSINESS?

Kids think about money, especially when we over-hear parents talking about it. They say stuff like, "I wonder when that check is coming?" and "I don't think we can go to that play tonight, it costs too much."

If you can't go somewhere or do something because of money, just tell your kids the truth. There's nothing to be ashamed of.

Kids should know what's going on about money, but not so much that we have to worry about not having a home or food or clothes.

24

We should also have some money of our own. If we go somewhere and see something for 95 cents, we should be able to buy it. But an allowance should be separate from chores. Kids should have to do stuff around the house just because we live there and should help keep it nice.

Having a little money teaches kids lessons. Like if you lose your dollar, you won't get another one. It teaches responsibility. And it teaches you to make good choices.

How much is a "little money"?

25

WHY ARE YOU ALWAYS TOO BUSY TO PLAY WITH ME?

I don't care if you're a mom or a dad — YOU STILL HAVE TO PLAY WITH YOUR KID.

I don't care if you can't remember any games — YOU STILL HAVE TO PLAY WITH YOUR KID.

I don't care if you're busy or you work full-time — YOU STILL HAVE TO PLAY WITH YOUR KID.

When you come home from work you're tired. You have a lot on your mind. You have to open the mail. Maybe you can lie down on your bed and play with your child there so you don't have to move. Or rent a video and watch it together.

27

It's not that hard. Pretend you're a child and think about what you liked back then. I know it's a long time ago but maybe you can get hypnotized.

Parents have to learn how to change from being an a-dult to a child. Here's how: Take off your business suit, sit on the floor, ignore the phone and make a fool of yourself.

It's important to work and make money. But your child is more important. If you don't play with us, we may learn to live without you. We may even run away some day and find someone else to play with.

I wish you knew how often I'd give anything to stop working and play with you. Because you DO matter more than my work. But I have to work in order to make money to buy food and clothes and send you to camp. It's hard to find a balance between work and play.

WHY DO SOME PEOPLE NOT LIKE IT THAT i'M JEWISH?

I have these two friends who aren't Jewish. One is from Korea and the other is just a real weird kid.

Once I was sitting across from them in the school lunch-room and they said they wouldn't talk to me because I was Jewish. I ignored them. It made me feel bad. Just because I'm Jewish doesn't mean I'm not normal.

Everyone should respect each other. Except Saddam Hussein.

People shouldn't be mean just because people are a different religion or color. Maybe they act that way because they were treated that way. Or because they're scared of the person who is different.

But it's good that the world is made up of so many different kinds of people. It's like a two-year-old's fingerpainting filled with all different colors and shapes.

If I was President, I'd give everyone one day off a year to go to a restaurant and talk to someone really different. I'd call it Peace Day.

Maybe we should even respect Saddam Hussein. Because the more we understand people who scare us, the better chance we have of building a peaceful world.

WHY DIDN'T YOU ASK ME IF i WANTED A LITTLE BROTHER?

When you have a new baby the bigger kid feels like he or she isn't getting enough attention. We don't feel as important anymore. For example, the baby is born and your dad runs and takes you to your Grandma's or a sitter's and just leaves you there and you feel all alone and you don't know when he'll come back and you don't understand what's happening.

Candy doesn't help in this situation.

But presents do. The baby gets lots of presents (and he can't even DO anything!) so make sure to get your bigger kid a present so she won't feel left out.

Talking helps too. Sit down and tell your child—a hundred times—what's happening. Say that you'll need to spend more time with the baby and you might get tired and crabby, but your love is still huge.

You can call the bigger kid "Very Important Big Sister," and buy a cute t-shirt. That's okay, as long as you don't forget about the feelings we have inside that maybe aren't so good about the baby.

If you feel bad that your bigger kid isn't excited about this baby, remember this: it may take 'til the year 4000, but someday we'll be friends.

SMART TIPS:

PUT your bigger kid in your lap and put the baby in their lap so they think they're holding the baby even though you're holding them.

IF the baby is screaming and your older kid wants to escape, make plans for them. If they're old enough, plan a sleepover so at least they can get one good night's sleep.

If you have three children, ask the oldest to explain to the middle what's going on since they were once that person. (But don't put them in charge... don't even let it happen by accident.)

great ideas!

WHY DID YOU AND DADDY GET DIVORCED?

Divorce is really hard for kids. It feels like someone's splitting your heart in two and Mom's on one side pulling and Dad's on the other and you feel so scared.

Kids whose parents divorce are scared of lots of things. We're scared we won't have anywhere to live. We're scared we'll have to choose. We're scared Mom and Dad will fight and we won't know what to do. We're scared that one of our parents will meet someone else and we'll be stuck with them.

Kids whose parents divorce are pretty mad, too.

37

If they could say what they wanted, they'd say: "I'm mad at you!!! It's not fair!! You don't have a right to do this because it hurts me, too!!"

And we worry that it's our fault. That maybe we fought too much with our brothers or sisters and that made our parents tense and then they started fighting.

Kids have schemes to get their parents back together, like pretending they're real sick. (I don't think it works very often, unless you have pneumonia or something.)

Sometimes it helps to talk about it to a Feelings Doctor. It's a good idea to tell your feelings to

Someone other than your parents so you don't hurt their feelings. I went to a support group at school, but my brother didn't want to. I think it should be the child's choice; they may not want to talk about their feelings with a stranger.

My parents got divorced last year. I don't like very much to think about the day they told me and Evan. But we're still a family... just a different kind of family.

 I'm so glad you know we're still a family. And, it breaks my heart to know how much Daddy and I have hurt you. We understand your fear. We accept your anger. Hopefully, in time we will all heal.

WHY WON'T YOU LET ME GO TO THE MALL WITH MY FRIENDS?

I know: Because I'm too young. Because I might get lost. Because someone might kidnap me and take me away.

There have to be limits, but it might be time to let your kids do a couple of things on their own.

If your child is two, he can go potty alone.

If your child is five, he can play in his room alone.

If your child is ten, he can talk on the phone alone.

Parents worry about letting kids go because they're scared we won't come back.

40

We will. You're our parents. You raised us. We look up to you.

We're not always going to be under your umbrella the rest of our lives, so we need to know what to do when it rains.

You can be too protective of children. If you are, we might grow up and think you're the only one we can trust. I have two older friends, Jill and Jan, who I talk to when I don't feel like talking to my Mom. It's always good to get a second opinion.

DON'T PUT A CAGE AROUND YOUR CHILD THAT'S STUCK TO YOU. Sometimes you need to leave us alone and sometimes you need to jump in. Maybe you and your child can figure out a certain eyeblink or sign that says: Help! I need you right now!

41

• HOW TO KNOW IF YOUR CHILD NEEDS YOUR HELP:

If we lock ourselves in our room.

IF we can't sleep.

IF we tell stupid jokes.

IF we hit something.

IF we tell lies.

IF we have a stomach ache.

IF we ask to go to bed early.

IF we refuse to watch television.

Remember when you used to give me detailed instructions on "babysitting" your dolly each morning before you left for kindergarten? That's how parents feel every single day. We'd do anything to keep you safe and dry beneath our umbrella.

DID I EVER DO SOMETHING TO MAKE YOU NOT LOVE ME?

Did you stop loving me when I went to my friend's house when you said I couldn't?

Did you stop loving me when I swore at you? Or didn't you hear me? (I kind of whispered it.)

A child can't survive if their parents don't love them. You disintegrate.

I know sometimes I do bad things, but that doesn't mean you should stop loving me. I'm still your child!

Parents should tell their kids they love them fourteen times a day. If they do something bad, you can say, "You did something bad and I'm going to have to punish you, but that doesn't make you a bad person or mean that I don't love you anymore."

And kids have to love their parents when they do something bad, too. It's only fair.

• SMART TALK:

Instead of saying, "I'm so mad at you I could kill you", say, "I still like you, but I'm angry about _____."

1. I LOVE YOU
2. I LOVE YOU
3. I LOVE YOU
4. I LOVE YOU
5. I LOVE YOU
6. I LOVE YOU
7. I LOVE YOU
8. I LOVE YOU
9. I LOVE YOU
10. I LOVE YOU
11. I LOVE YOU
12. I LOVE YOU
13. I LOVE YOU
14. I LOVE YOU

WHY DO YOU YELL SO MUCH?

Parents yell when they're angry. They yell because they think it's the only way to get their kids to pay attention, but it's not. Or else it's because their own parents yelled at them.

When parents yell, it makes kids cry. We feel like we're just a tiny little person and we don't know why everyone's screaming.

Put it this way—I sometimes get frightened. It's awful being frightened of your parents. They're supposed to protect you.

47

Kids usually feel like screaming back, but don't because then their parents will scream more. It makes us scared you'll lose control and hit us.

Sometimes you have to yell to get your message across. But if you're always screaming, your kids will tune you out and pretend their deaf.

But you shouldn't ever hit. Here's my DON'T HIT YOUR KID RAP:

Never hit your kid
Or kick, kick, kick
Just don't do it
Cause it's sick, sick, sick.

48

Keep your hands to yourself
Use your words instead
And keep them nice
Or I'll send you to bed.

If your kid needs work
Then do it with love
Just remember there's someone
Watching from above.

If you're mean to your kids
We'll hold up a mirror
And all you'll see
Is hate and fear.

Try time out
Or take away a treat
But never, ever
beat, beat, beat.

If you're out of control
Then get some rest.
And pretty soon
You'll be back to your best.

Parents feel awful when they hit their kids
So why do they do it? Because they're stressed
out. Frustrated. Out of control. None of which
is a good reason. I fervently hope that someday we'll live in a world where parents never
hit their children for any reason, under any
circumstance.

DO YOUR RICE KRISPIES TALK TO YOU?

Most kids are picky eaters. We like to pick what we eat.

Some parents say: "If you don't eat your dinner there's no food until breakfast."

Do they want you to starve?

It's not fair because maybe we're not hungry right now.

51

So save it. Leave it on the table and when we're ready we'll eat it. If we don't, it will be breakfast. Cold tuna casserole is great in the morning!

Don't bribe your kids with food. If you say, "If you're good, I'll give you a cookie," we'll always expect a cookie when we're good even when we're grown up and run a good meeting.

But junk food is worth being good for. It's sparkly. But sometimes it makes us tired or crazy or gives us a bad stomach ache.

If you give kids too much junk food, we won't grow. If you NEVER let kids eat junk food, it will make us feel stupid at birthday parties or school. We'll feel like a dweeb.

A little is fine.

Some kids like putting on fancy clothes and going out to a restaurant and sitting with their legs crossed and not making a peep. There's good food, but you have to wait, so I like places that give you crackers.

BUT NO SALAD! Salad is what they give you while they're making you wait for the real food.

I very much do recommend places that give kids meals in toy airplanes or cars with treats like animal crackers inside.

- ## SMART TIPS:

1. GIVE HEALTHY CHOICES. Offer them chicken or meatloaf, so even if both make them sick, at least they get to choose.

2. ADD SUGAR. Put sugar or maple syrup on grapefruit or marshmallows on carrots.

3. BRING TOYS TO RESTAURANTS.

I'll make you a deal. For the next month, you can make dinner every night. Be sure what you serve is delicious and nutritious and I'll promise to eat everything on my plate. Okay?

WHEN WILL DADDY START WEARING HIS SEAT BELT?

Here's a conversation between a kid and his father. The kid's name is Tommy. The father is Daddy.

TOMMY: Dad, when are you going to start wearing your seat belt?

DAD: I don't need to, Tommy. I'm just fine this way.

TOMMY: Really Dad, you should. Today, Safety the Seatbelt came to our school. He gave us a packet on wearing seat belts. I read it and you really should, Dad, it will save your life!

DAD: Well, all right, Tommy. Thanks a lot.

When parents forget or are too busy, then kids have to remind them to do the right thing. Parents give lectures like, "Look both ways before you cross the street." Sometimes kids have to give lectures too, like reminding their parents to recycle or drive carefully or watch their cholestral. Because kids worry about parents just like parents worry about kids.

 Thanks for reminding us!

DO YOU THINK I'M POPULAR?

Friends are your life. When your parents like your friends and your friends like your parents it's dandy. You feel like a piece of candy.

But when your parents don't like your friends and your friends don't like your parents you feel like a piece of eggplant. And if you've ever cooked eggplant and cut it open, you know there isn't much inside.

That's how you feel — Flat. Empty. Black and blue.

You need to treat your kids friends well, even if you don't like them, don't make a big deal of it. Because they might just be passing through the kitchen.

guess what? Parents really want their kids' friends to like them, too. Then we feel comfortable, especially if we run into them in the kitchen.

Have you ever had sex?

Kids wonder if their parents have sex. Obviously, the answer is yes, because you're alive.

I think once is enough, unless you want two children.

Kids have trouble imagining parents having sex. Why do you do it? What's the big deal?

Thinking about sex is kinda gross...and scary. One thing's definately important — parents should lock their door if they're having sex, so kids won't walk in.

Actually, kids aren't that interested. We're curious, but if you really stop to think about it, it feels icky.

Kids wonder if their parents have kissed someone else or if you wish you were married to another person. Or if their parents have had an affair. I'm not sure I want the answer to this. If it's no, it doesn't matter, and if it's yes, I don't want to know.

Marriage is hard because you have to do things you don't want to do, like watch wrestling or eat brussel sprouts just because your husband or wife wants to. You have to compromise.

Marriage is hard! And as far as sex goes, it's not icky at all. In fact, it's quite wonderful, as long as you wait for the right person and the right time.

WHY CAN'T I PUT YOU IN TIME OUT ?

You can put me in time out when I do something wrong, so why can't I put you in time out when YOU do something wrong.

Parents should be put in time out when:
1. They abuse their kids.
2. They scream and scream.
3. They don't listen.
4. They say you can't do things that you're perfectly capable of if you just try.

Parents should learn how it feels to be put in time out.

61

It's boring. You end up thinking you can't do anything right.

The reason parents don't get put in time out is
because they're in charge. This started a long time
ago. In the beginning of time, grown-ups ruled the
world, so now parents rule everything. The power
was passed down.

It would make more sense if kids had more power.
There was a twelve-year-old boy in the newspaper
last week who divorced his parents because
they were bad to him. The judge gave him
new parents. I think the judge was right.

 So do I. That boy's parents needed worse consequences than time-out and he needed and deserved better parents. let's hope he'll be safe and happy in his new home.

WHY ARE YOU SO NOSY?

Parents shouldn't butt in, unless they think there's something wrong, like their kid is taking drugs.

Kids need privacy for lots of reasons. Like if we're frustrated because the Nintendo isn't working and we need to go in our room and hit the bed. Or maybe we just need to be alone to think, to read, to dream, or just to be.

We might need to be alone with our private parts. So knock on the door before you come in.

Kids also need privacy with our thoughts. Parents always want to know what's going on, like, "What happened at school today?" But their kid might not want to say. We might feel like, "Get out of my life, Buddy," if you ask too many questions. I mean, you've gotta have your parents in your life, to take you to the doctor and that kind of thing, but we also need our own life.

Kids also need privacy when their friends are over. That doesn't mean we're doing anything bad. We just don't want to be bothered by our parents or our brother or sister.

This may hurt your feelings. But your kids DO need privacy because when we're all grown up we may need it in other ways, so this is good practice.

Here's the other side of the story: Kids need — and deserve — privacy. But parents need to know what's going on in their kids' lives. We feel shut out when you don't let us in. We worry. And we care.

WHY DO YOU MAKE ME READ BOOKS ABOUT SEX AND PERIODS?

Kids know more about these things than you think we do.

Don't you think we talk about it with our friends?

Don't you think we learn about it in school?

Don't you think we play "doctor" and "house"?

Talking about this stuff is embarrassing. When your parents have a "talk" with you about the birds and the bees, you wish you could turn into a bird or a bee and fly up to the top of a tree. You don't mind hearing it, you just don't want them to look at you and say it at the same time.

Face it. When you-know-who has a you-know-what with you-know-who cause you-know-why, you really don't want to hear you-know-what, especially from your parents, cause you already know.

I suppose sometimes parents have to have "talks", so do it when your kid is nine or ten, so they get it through their head before they're a teenager and are already doing it. And be sure their favorite parent is the one to talk to them about it and take them somewhere they like — a park or the mall — so they have fun while you're talking to them.

Sex is dumb and boring. When I get to boring parts of a book I just skip over them. If I was reading this book instead of writing it, I'd skip over this part for sure.

Kids really don't care that much about sex. If we want to know more we'll ask. Okay?

 Okay.

WAS I A MISTAKE?

Did you want me? Did you mean to have me? Do you ever wish you hadn't had me?

Sometimes I wish I didn't have you. Like when I'm mad or sad or want different parents.

Sometimes I dream about having two other people as my parents. Parents who don't work but still get money. Who tutor me so I don't have to go to school. And I'd like a different brother and sister every single day.

If your kid was a mistake, tell her you're extra glad to have her as your kid. If she wasn't a mistake, be sure to tell her because it will make her feel great.

 Daddy and I wanted you more than anything in the world.

WHY DO YOU MAKE ME WEAR THINGS I HATE?

Kids worry that other kids will make fun of them if they're wearing stupid clothes. Sometimes parents should be able to tell you what to wear, like if you're going to church or temple and you wanna wear old grubby jeans. But when parents force you to wear something you don't like, you feel insecure, unhappy, and uncomfortable in two ways: because what you're wearing doesn't FEEL good and YOU don't feel good inside.

My mom and I fight about what I wear. I call her the "Clothes Police." Sometimes I get mad when she makes me wear things I don't want to wear like the black t-shirt with the roses. She bought it because she likes it. I think it's ugly.

If she wants me to wear something to school because she thinks it's cute and I pick out something else and she still says "no", then I get mad. I feel bad inside when we fight. It gives me a stomach-ache.

Parents make a big deal out of clothes because they want to impress their friends. But your friends aren't really your friends if they like you less because your kid isn't dressed up.

Personally, I think life would be a lot easier if everyone went naked. Then we wouldn't have this problem.

 Easy for you to say, sweetie. You don't have any stretch marks.

WOULD YOU LOVE ME IF I WAS DUMB?

I'm not saying anyone is dumb, but sometimes if kids do bad in school, we worry that our parents will be mad at us.

We feel pressured. Sometimes you think you're cheering your kid on by saying: "Go get 100 on that test", but they think you're really saying: "You HAVE to get 100 on that test." Then they go to school and they don't get 100 and they feel like they're letting you down.

It's really scary to let your parents down.

It's fine to encourage kids, but be sure to let them know it's okay not to get 100.

Or take violin playing, for example. You can say: "Would you like to play the violin? I played it and it was fun." But if your kid says "No. I want to play the trombone," you have to accept it.

Parents have the right to have some expectations, but not to the point where everything has to be perfect!

Sometimes parents pretend they're perfect. So it would help to know if you've ever flunked a test.

If I did, I'd definately be scared to tell you, so if I knew it happened to you, too, I might feel better. It helps to know I'm not the only one who makes mistakes.

Mistakes are good because you learn from them. I'd never make a wish to be perfect because then I wouldn't learn anything. And I wouldn't wish for the world to be perfect either, because it wouldn't be as exciting. Like if the world was perfect, your car wouldn't break down and you wouldn't end up lost in the middle of no-where which is an adventure.

It's much better to know that mistakes and problems are okay. Making them doesn't have to be the end of the world.

Joe, I once failed a statistics test, but I was too scared to tell my parents. I hope you can always come to me and share your struggles and your triumphs. I'll love you either way.

81

ARE YOU AFRAID TO DIE?

Kids are afraid of their parents dying because they don't know who they'll live with. It would be especially horrible if your parents died while you were at school because you wouldn't know where to go after school.

Sometimes grown-ups think kids shouldn't go to funerals, but that's wrong. It keeps kids away from life. And reality.

When I was five my Papa Lester died. He used to take me to Embers on Sunday mornings. He'd give the waitress $5.00 to take me to the bathroom.

82

But then he died. Before he died I wrote him a good-bye letter. It was buried with him, but my Nanny Jane still wrote me back.

Before Papa's funeral, the Rabbi read me a book called, "Freddie the Leaf." It's a good book to read to kids at funerals. I highly recommend it.

What I really know about death is that people have nine lives like cats so they come back. I'd like to come back as a grown-up so I wouldn't have a bedtime.

I have a funny feeling you've ALREADY been a grown-up!

83

WHEN WILL YOU STOP SMOKING?

This is a big worry, because you'll kill yourself. We're also afraid for ourselves because second-hand smoke is bad for you, too.

Besides, it smells.

My friend, Jason and I had this idea: Take your parents' pack of cigarettes and remove all the cigarettes and flush them down the toilet. Then, write encouraging notes on little pieces of white paper, roll them up and put them back in the pack. Notes like: "Keep up the good work, Mom!" and, "Stop smoking. It's not good for you, love Zoe."

I won't ever start smoking because I don't wanna ruin my lungs. And it's a very bad example to children.

Speaking of examples, parents need to remember that they're role models. Kids look up to parents and admire them, so if you smoke or swear your kid may follow in your footsteps.

You may not know this but kids watch their parents all the time. We see everything. So if there's something you don't want your kids to do, DON'T DO IT.

It must be hard for you to watch me smoke (although you must admit, I hardly ever swear!) Like kids, parents are great in some ways and need improvement in others. It takes time and courage to change bad habits. Please be patient.

IF GOD CAN SEE EVERTHING WHY DOESN'T HE TELL ME WHEN MY BROTHER'S ABOUT TO TRASH MY ROOM?

I think God's the everlasting mosquito. He always comes back but he never bites.

Actually, I think God is half man, half woman. One leg has hair and the other wears pantyhose.

Do you know what else I know about God? I think God's really ugly. But it doesn't matter because we can't see God. And if God's ugly, it makes all the ugly people feel more beautiful.

People pray about the things they want. I pray for two things: To be famous. And to not get hit by a car.

I don't understand why we pray to God. Why don't we just pray to each other?

 I pray that you and I will always be able to talk to each other this way.